MYSTERIOUS JOY

SMALL GROUP WORKBOOK

Icebreakers, Discussion Questions & an Answer Key

EDWIN R. RIDEOUT,
THD., MDIV., MA., B.TH.

Mysterious Joy: Life in the Kingdom of God

Contact author via email:

edwinrhoda@gmail.com

www.edwinrideout.com

Facebook: www.facebook.com/edwin.r.rideout/

Linkedin: www.linkedin.com/in/edwinrideout

X (Twitter): twitter.com/edwinrideout

Instagram: www.instagram.com/edwin.r.rideout/

Phone (780)742-3933

Published by: Hemingway Publishers

About The Author

In September 2008, Edwin and Rhoda began their ministry at Family Christian Centre (FCC), leading the church into a season of remarkable growth and expansion. Together, they have championed visionary initiatives such as the Legacy Counselling Centre, the Wheaton-Penney Childcare Centre, Mercy Ministry, and the planting of over twenty churches among unreached people groups in Nepal and India. These initiatives reflect their unwavering commitment to cultivating strong, healthy communities both locally and globally.

Known for his boundless energy and unwavering passion, Edwin is a vibrant presence within the congregation and the broader community. His preaching and teaching style are characterized by directness and relatability, echoing the heartfelt desire for people to encounter Christ and embark on a transformative journey of discipleship.

Edwin's educational journey is a testament to his commitment to the ministry. He earned a Bachelor of Theology from Master's College and Seminary in Toronto, Ontario; a Master of Divinity from Oral Roberts University in Tulsa, Oklahoma; a Master of Arts from Acadia University in Kentville, Nova Scotia; and a Doctor of Theology from Gateway International Bible Institute. His scholarly background underscores his dedication to spiritual growth and leadership.

He hosts a weekly podcast, **_Encountering the Divine_**, _airing in 190 nations via._ Holy Spirit Broadcasting Network, KITV Network, and Global Fire TV. He is consistently in the top ten most viewed. He has spoken nationally across Canada at various churches and camps. He has also spoken internationally in the United States, Ethiopia, Malawi, Thailand, Nepal, Rwanda, the United Arab Emirates, the Dominican Republic, Siberia, and Sri Lanka.

Edwin and his wife, Rhoda, live in Fort McMurray, Alberta. They have three adult children—Shane (married to Cindy), Amanda (married to Leroy), and Matthew (married to Carla)—and are proud grandparents to five grandchildren: Abigail, Liam, Silas, Jaxson, and Levi.

Table of Contents

Introduction

In a world often consumed by self-interest and material gain, Edwin R. Rideout invites you on a transformative journey into the heart of *Kingdom living*—a life marked by meaning, generosity, and divine purpose. *Mysterious Joy: Life in the Kingdom of God* explores the profound rewards of selfless giving and the enduring happiness that comes from living according to Kingdom values.

Drawing on personal experiences and timeless wisdom, Edwin explores the essence of holy actions and how they proclaim the reality and priorities of God's Kingdom. He reminds us of Jesus' radical words—challenging us to love our enemies, do good to those who hate us, and give without expecting anything in return—all hallmarks of Kingdom citizenship.

Through captivating storytelling and insightful reflections, he unveils the barriers that often hinder a generous spirit—whether it's the hoarding mindset of our culture, doubts about those in need, or fears of not having enough. He skillfully guides us toward a Kingdom perspective, where even modest acts of kindness carry eternal significance.

With real-life examples, including the inspiring generosity of historical figures such as John Wesley and David Green, *Mysterious Joy: Life in the Kingdom of God* demonstrates the transformative power of Kingdom generosity—enriching our faith, deepening our trust in God, and bringing lasting joy. It calls us to embody the Kingdom ethic: to love God with all our heart, soul, and mind, and to love our neighbor as ourselves.

Join Edwin on this extraordinary journey from fear to fearlessness, and experience the mysterious joy of living generously in the Kingdom of God. You will be inspired to live a life that counts—for time and for eternity.

If you love those who love you, what credit is that to you? For even sinners love those who love them. And if you do good to those who do good to you, what credit is that to you? For even sinners do the same. And if you lend to those from whom you expect to receive, what credit is that to you? Even sinners lend to sinners in order to receive back the same amount. But love your enemies and do good, and lend, expecting nothing in return; and your reward will be great, and you will be sons of the Most High; for He Himself is kind to ungrateful and evil people. Be merciful, just as your Father is merciful (Luke 6:32-36 NASV).

Format

An ideal small group Bible study experience incorporates several vital elements to nurture spiritual growth and community among its members. Furthermore, a practical small group teaching experience imparts knowledge and inspires curiosity, critical thinking, and a lifelong love of learning. I encourage you to create a small-group experience characterized by:

A Prayerful Foundation:

Begin and conclude with prayer, inviting God's presence and guidance into the group's study and discussions, setting a tone of reverence, and seeking divine wisdom.

Engaging Scripture-based Study:

Focus on reading and discussing the study material, emphasizing the scriptural element. Encourage members to delve into the depths of Scripture, share their insights, and apply biblical truths to their lives. Aim to foster an interactive environment that encourages questions and reflections.

Worship and Praise:

This time includes praise, whether through music, shared testimonies, or reading psalms, to uplift the group's spirit and foster a deeper connection with God.

Fellowship and Community Building:

Provides opportunities for members to share personal experiences, support one another in prayer, and build meaningful relationships, thereby strengthening community and fostering a sense of belonging.

Service and Outreach:

Encourage the practical application of the study through acts of service within the group or broader community, embodying the teachings of Jesus through compassion and action.

A Relaxed and Welcoming Atmosphere:

Maintain a casual and inviting environment where members feel comfortable and valued. Foster open dialogue and genuine connections, regardless of one's faith journey.

Chapter 1
Fearful to Fearless

I was a reluctant giver until I met the one who generously gave me eternal life,

Jesus Christ.

Oh, the depth of the riches and wisdom and knowledge of God! How unsearchable are his judgments and how inscrutable his ways! For who has known the mind of the Lord, or who has been his counselor? Or who has given a gift to him that he might be repaid? For from him and through him and to him are all things. To him be glory forever. Amen (Romans 11:33-36 ESV).

ICEBREAKERS

A Truth and a Fear:

Each person shares a true statement about themselves and one fear they've overcome or are working to overcome. This breaks the ice and immediately opens up a dialogue about fears in a personal and relatable way (2 minutes each).

Biblical Courage Quotes:

Prepare cards with different Bible verses about courage and fearlessness (e.g., Joshua 1:9, Isaiah 41:10). Each member draws a card, reads the scripture aloud, and briefly shares what it means to them or how it could apply to their life.

"Would You Rather" - Courage Edition:

Pose a series of "Would you rather" questions that involve choosing between a comfortable action and one that requires courage. This light-hearted approach can lead to deeper discussions about the nature of fear and courage.

Pass the Fear Parcel:

Wrap a small, light-hearted gift many times in different layers of wrapping paper. Between each layer, place a prompt related to overcoming fear or encouraging courage. As the parcel is passed around (with music playing in the background, if possible), when the music stops, the person holding the parcel unwraps a layer and answers the prompt. Continue until the gift is revealed.

GO DEEPER

Key Text: Malachi 3:8–12 ESV

A. We were born into a world tainted by sin and death, resulting in our understanding of God and true life being inherently imperfect. In Matthew 18:3, Jesus emphasizes the necessity of adopting a childlike attitude to discover the life within God's kingdom. In Colossians 3:10 (NASV), Paul used present continuing Greek verbiage to describe the redeeming process, "and have put on the new self, which is being renewed to a true knowledge according to the image of the One who created it."

Read Colossians 3:1–17. Identify steps necessary to live authentically.

Example: Set your mind on the things that are above, not on the things that are on earth.

____

____

B. People sometimes think of giving and generosity as relating only to money. "Luke 6:45–47 (VOICE) reads,

> "It's the same with people. A person full of goodness in his heart produces good things; a person with an evil reservoir in his heart pours out evil things. The heart overflows in the words a person speaks; your words reveal what's within your heart. What good is it to mouth the words, "Lord! Lord!" if you don't live by My teachings? What matters is that you come to Me, hear My words, and actually live by them."

Earlier in this chapter, I discussed various indulgences and actions people engage in to find peace and significance. The widow from the 1 Kings 17 narrative was no different. In her eyes, her life depended on the small amount of oil and wheat in her cupboard. However, she found real life when Elijah requested that she relinquish her vital supplies. Can you identify two other similar examples of this outlook in the Bible?

____

____

____

Illustration to Ponder:

For vampire bats, the mark of true friendship is breaking bread—er, blood—together. These animals require their liquid blood meals to survive, and they need them often. If one misses a feeding just three nights in a row, it could starve to death. They have developed a friendly way to cope; well-fed bats regurgitate blood directly into the mouths of hungry companions. That blood may not be enough for a full meal, but it provides enough substance for the recipient to live and hunt another day.[1]

A Practical Action:

Together with a significant other and the Holy Spirit, make a careful inventory of your life priorities. The goal is to evaluate where serving others fits in the grand scheme of your life.

Additional Observations:

---

[1]   https://www.scientificamerican.com/article/blood-ties-vampire-bats-build-trust-to-become-food-sharing-pals/.

Chapter 2
Scrap Your Plans. God Has Bigger Ones.

When the plans of God are hitched to pain, we are sustained by His grace.

So he departed from there and found Elisha the son of Shaphat, who was plowing with twelve yoke of oxen in front of him, and he was with the twelfth. Elijah passed by him and cast his cloak upon him. And he left the oxen and ran after Elijah and said, "Let me kiss my father and my mother, and then I will follow you." And he said to him, "Go back again, for what have I done to you?" And he returned from following him and took the yoke of oxen and sacrificed them and boiled their flesh with the yokes of the oxen and gave it to the people, and they ate. Then he arose and went after Elijah and assisted him (1 Kings 19:19–21 ESV).

ICEBREAKERS

Dream Sharing Circle:

Invite participants to share a dream or plan they once had for their life that didn't materialize. Then, if applicable, they can share how something unexpected God brought into their life was better than their original plan. This encourages openness and reflection on God's providence (2 minutes each).

God's Bigger Plans Charades:

Prepare slips of paper with Bible stories that exemplify how God's bigger plans surpass individual plans (e.g., Joseph becoming governor of Egypt, Moses leading the Israelites, and Esther becoming queen). Participants act out the stories without speaking, and the rest of the group attempts to guess the story. This activity is fun and a powerful reminder of God's sovereignty.

The "If I Were" Game:

Ask participants to complete the sentence, "If I were in charge of the world, I would..." This can lead to humorous responses, but it should transition into a discussion on why God's sovereignty and His plans are perfect, given our limited understanding.

GO DEEPER

Key Text: 1 Kings 19:19–21 NASB

A. Elisha's self-abandonment mirrors Jesus, who temporarily forsook heavenly glories to serve humanity, living solely for total obedience to God's will, even unto death. In Luke 14:12–14, while dining at a Pharisee's house, Jesus encourages his audience to invite those society neglects, assuring that blessings will be returned at the resurrection. He warns against forming self-serving connections, urging us to give generously without expecting anything in return. This way, by practicing self-abandonment, we emulate Christ and secure eternal rewards. Find two more examples of similar teachings.

____

____

____

B. Nearly 400 years ago, a group of Puritan leaders produced *The Westminster Shorter Catechism*, a summary device designed to teach the fundamental doctrines of Christianity. It is laid out as a series of questions and answers. The first question: *What is the chief end of man?* In other words, *what is the great purpose of our individual lives?* The answer provided—"**Man's chief end is to glorify God and to enjoy Him forever.**" Can you identify two characters in the Bible who set such an example for us?

____

____

____

Illustration to Ponder:

Beavers build dams to sustain their lives. Those same dams create deep pools and channels, creating unique worlds for fish and millions of water creatures. The deep pools and channels create drought-proof landscapes and wetlands to refresh moose, deer, elk, and birds. The open spaces they create in the woodland canopy allow sunlight to penetrate, creating a warm and shallow aquatic habitat around the edges of ponds for wildlife and insects.

A Practical Action:

Ask God to help you become more conscious of others' needs. Also, inquire how you may appropriately respond to those needs. Create a journal to document your identified needs and your response to those needs.

Additional Observations:

8

Chapter 3
Uncomfortably Obedient

Obedience is the sustaining agency of Holiness.

Trust in the Lord with all your heart,

and do not lean on your own understanding.

In all your ways acknowledge him,

and he will make straight your paths.

(Proverbs 3:5–6 ESV)

ICEBREAKERS

Uncomfortable Commands Sorting Hat:

Write down various burdensome commands or teachings from the Bible on slips of paper (e.g., love your enemies, give without expecting return, forgive repeatedly). Let participants draw a slip and briefly discuss their feelings about that command and its challenges (2 minutes each).

Obedience in Action Stories:

Ask group members to think of a time when they witnessed someone's obedience to God that initially seemed uncomfortable or challenging but resulted in something positive. Sharing these stories can inspire and remind everyone of the power of obedience (2 minutes each).

Blindfold Trust Walk:

In a safe, open space, pair up participants for a blindfolded walk where one guides the blindfolded partner using only their voice. This physical representation of trust and obedience can open conversations about the discomfort and faith involved in being spiritually obedient.

The Jonah Run:

Jonah's initial refusal to follow God's command offers a relatable story of resistance before obedience. Have participants share a brief "Jonah moment" from their lives—when they tried to run from what God called them to do—and what happened (2 minutes each).

GO DEEPER

Key Text: Proverbs 3:5–6 (ESV)

A. King Solomon challenged his subjects to trust the Lord and never make decisions based on their observations. He promised that God would care for their future if they lived life from that perspective. How does such a perspective affect the way you live your life?

____

____

B. Abraham responded obediently to God's request. Can you identify at least two actions you've sensed God asking of you?

____

____

C. Write the results of your obedience or disobedience in these actions.

____

____

Illustration to Ponder:

Motivation in dog training falls into three basic categories: Pleasure, Paycheck, and Penalty

Pleasure: All living things naturally move towards comfort and away from discomfort. Your dog is no exception and will engage in each behavior simply for pleasure.

Paycheck: Dogs are motivated by a paycheck. Rover may love you, but he may also love chasing squirrels. A paycheck, such as a ball or doggy biscuits, leverages the likelihood that he will choose to engage with you when he'd rather do something else.

Penalty: Negative consequences are also powerful motivators. By introducing an unpleasant stimulus, like a verbal reprimand, your dog will avoid some behaviors because it does not enjoy the outcome.

A Practical Action:

Ask God what next step(s) you can take to grow your dependency on Him. Journal the process.

Additional Observations:

____

____

____

Chapter 4
The Storm Which Released a Blessing

Our crisis is God's springboard. He is exceedingly resourceful.

When a moderate south wind came up, thinking that they had attained their purpose, they weighed anchor and began sailing along Crete, closer to shore. But before very long a violent wind, called Euraquilo, rushed down from the land; and when the ship was caught in it and could not head up into the wind, we gave up and let ourselves be driven by the wind. Running under the shelter of a small island called Cauda, we were able to get the ship's boat under control only with difficulty. After they had hoisted it up, they used supporting cables in undergirding the ship; and fearing that they might run aground on the shallows of Syrtis, they let down the sea anchor and let themselves be driven along in this way. The next day as we were being violently tossed by the storm, they began to jettison the cargo; and on the third day they threw the ship's tackle overboard with their own hands. Since neither sun nor stars appeared for many days, and no small storm was assailing us, from then on all hope of our being saved was slowly abandoned (Acts 27:13–20 NASB).

The Storm Which Released a Blessing

ICEBREAKERS

Blessing Raindrops:

On pieces of paper cut into raindrop shapes, ask group members to write down blessings in their lives that came from difficult situations. Hang these raindrops on a string or board as a visual reminder of storms' blessings, fostering a positive outlook on trials.

Storm Stories:

Invite members to share a brief personal story about a difficult "storm" that eventually led to an unexpected blessing or lesson learned. This can help create a bond of shared experience and set the tone for the study's theme (2 minutes each).

Guess the Storm:

Prepare brief descriptions of biblical stories where a character goes through a metaphorical or literal storm and comes out with a blessing (e.g., Jonah and the whale, Paul's shipwreck on Malta). Have participants guess the story or character based on the description. This activity can highlight the theme's biblical roots.

GO DEEPER

Key Text: Acts 27:13–20 (NASB)

Genesis 26:12–14 informs us, "Isaac sowed seed in the land in the time of famine." Trusting God for a 100-fold return on our investments—mercy, forgiveness, finances—during spiritual famine requires steadfast faith in God.

In Matthew 13:23 and Mark 4:20, Jesus said, those who hear the Word, understand it, receive, accept, and welcome it, will bear fruit—

some yielding 30-fold, some 60-fold, and some 100-fold. Identify two similar examples of teachings by Jesus.

____

____

____

Living generously in seasons of lack requires unwavering faith in God. When it appears we are in over our heads, we must seize hold of hope. Even those with an extensive faith reservoir may waver when adversities never let up. The Bible presents methods for increasing our faith. Luke 17:5 is an example. On that occasion, Jesus' followers asked Him to increase their faith. Can you identify at least two more?

____

Illustration to Ponder:

Bison and cows face storms differently. Storms in North America almost always brew from the west and roll out toward the east. When cows sense the storm coming from the west, they run toward the east. The problem is that cows aren't fast.

The storm catches up with them rather quickly. They attempt to outrun the storm. Instead, they run along with it, maximizing the energy required.

Bison react differently. They wait for the storm to cross over the crest of the mountaintop. As the storm rolls over the ridge, they turn and charge directly into it. By running at the storm, they run straight through it, minimizing the energy they expend during the storm.

A Practical Action:

Start a Prayer and Praise Journal. When spiritual obstacles confront us and we feel overwhelmed by our problems, we can forget what God has done for us.

A practical way to help us stay focused during such seasons is to document our prayer journey. Write prayer requests in a journal, including the date we entrusted them to God. When God answers our prayer, enter a praise report. Keep the journal for future reference. It will be a device to encourage our families and friends.

Additional Observations:

____

____

____

Chapter 5
Generosity—A Mode of Spiritual Warfare

Spiritual warfare is not a covert operation assigned to a few super-spiritual Christians. It occurs naturally as we respond obediently to the voice of the Holy Spirit.

For the desires of the flesh are against the Spirit, and the desires of the Spirit are against the flesh, for these are opposed to each other, to keep you from doing the things you want to do (Galatians 5:17 ESV).

ICEBREAKERS

Generosity Brainstorm:

Ask each member to quickly list as many acts of generosity as possible in one minute. Afterward, share and discuss how each act can positively impact and potentially counteract negativity or spiritual darkness.

The Generosity Challenge:

Propose a hypothetical scenario in which each person has an abundance of a specific resource (time, money, skills). Ask, "How would you use this resource to wage spiritual warfare through generosity?" This thought exercise encourages creative thinking about using what we have for spiritual good (2 minutes each).

Generosity—A Mode of Spiritual Warfare

Scriptural Treasure Hunt:

Prepare cards with Bible verses about generosity, giving, and spiritual warfare. Have participants draw cards, find and read the verse to the group, and discuss how each verse connects generosity with spiritual strength and warfare.

Personal Testimonies of Generosity:

Invite group members to share a brief story about a time when someone's generosity toward them significantly impacted their lives, especially during difficult times. This personal sharing can highlight the transformative power of generosity (2 minutes each).

GO DEEPER

Key Text: Galatians 5:17 (ESV)

A. In Galatians 5, Paul highlights the internal struggle believers experience between their sinful nature, often referred to as the flesh and the transformative work of the Holy Spirit. The flesh represents the fallen human nature, prone to selfishness, sinful desires, and actions that are contrary to God's will. On the other hand, the Spirit represents God's indwelling presence in believers' lives, leading them toward righteousness, holiness, and obedience to God's commands. How is this conflict expressed in generous living?

B. Paul's reminder to the Galatian believers encourages us to be mindful of the ongoing battle and to rely on the Holy Spirit's power and guidance. Find two scriptures that inform us how to do this.

Generosity—A Mode of Spiritual Warfare

Illustration to Ponder:

A caterpillar transforms into a butterfly through metamorphosis. Such a transformation is like spiritual warfare. The caterpillar represents a person undergoing spiritual struggle and transformation, while the emergence of a beautiful butterfly symbolizes victory and spiritual rebirth.

A Practical Action:

1. Prayerfully evaluate your current financial contributions to the work of Christ's Church. Inspect your income, expenses, and savings, then establish clear and measurable goals for your increased financial generosity.

2. Consider consulting with a Christian financial advisor or leaders within your faith community for guidance on financial stewardship and generosity. They can provide insights, wisdom, and support as you endeavor to increase your giving.

Additional Observations:

____

____

____

Chapter 6
The Fruit of Generosity

Generosity profoundly affects both the giver and the recipient. It kindles joy in the giver's soul and nourishes the receiver.

Whoever brings blessing will be enriched, and one who waters will himself be watered (Proverbs 11:25 ESV).

ICEBREAKERS

Generosity Circle:

Start by passing around a basket of fruit, with each type of fruit representing a different aspect of generosity (e.g., an apple for giving time, a banana for sharing resources, etc.). Participants pick fruit and share a personal experience or hope related to the aspect of generosity it represents (2 minutes each).

Acts of Generosity Bingo:

Create bingo cards filled with various acts of generosity (e.g., complimenting someone, making a donation, volunteering). Participants mark off what they've done recently. The first to get a line shares one of their experiences. This game highlights the many ways to practice generosity.

The Generosity Web:

Stand in a circle and hold a ball of yarn. Start by sharing an act of generosity you've experienced or done, then hold onto the end of the yarn and toss the ball to another person. Continue until everyone is connected by the web of yarn, illustrating how generosity connects and supports a community.

Generosity Quotes:

Prepare and distribute slips of paper with quotes about generosity from various sources, including Scripture. Each participant reads their quote aloud and briefly reflects on its meaning or how it resonates with them. This can provide diverse perspectives on generosity.

The Generosity Challenge:

As an icebreaker, challenge each group member to devise one act of generosity they can commit to performing before the next meeting. Share these commitments with the group. Participants can share their experiences and reflections on the challenge at the next meeting.

GO DEEPER

Key Text: Proverbs 11:25 (ESV)

A. Proverbs 11:25 says, "Whoever brings blessing will be enriched, and one who waters will himself be watered." Jesus taught the same principle in Luke 6:38. Can you think of two examples in the Bible where this principle is demonstrated?

____

____

B. Job's friends sat in silence with him for seven days. In some ancient cultures, there was a tradition of observing a period of mourning or silent contemplation when encountering great suffering or tragedy. Share some examples of related best practices from your culture.

____

____

Illustration to Ponder:

Oxpeckers perch on the backs or bodies of large mammals and consume external parasites, such as ticks, fleas, and lice, as well as dead skin and wounds. By feeding on these parasites, the oxpeckers help keep the mammal's skin free from harmful organisms and assist in wound healing. In return, the mammals provide the oxpeckers with a steady food source and a convenient perch from which to feed. This symbiotic relationship benefits both the oxpeckers and the large mammals. The oxpeckers receive a source of nutrition and gain protection from predators while feeding on parasites. The large mammals, in turn, benefit from removing bothersome parasites and potential assistance in wound care, leading to improved hygiene and possibly reduced disease transmission.

A Practical Action:

Provide simple acts of kindness for several people this week. It can have a significant impact. Hold the door open for someone, offer to help carry groceries, mow someone's lawn, or cook a meal for an older person or a student. Consider performing random acts of kindness, like leaving uplifting notes for others to find.

Additional Observations:

Chapter 7
Our Capacity for Significance

Words have the capability to uplift others and create a more compassionate and empathetic world—one where individuals are inspired to succeed.

We are his workmanship, created in Christ Jesus for good works, which God prepared beforehand, that we should walk in them (Ephesians 2:10 ESV).

ICEBREAKERS

Inspirational Figures:

Ask individuals to briefly talk about someone they admire for their significant contributions to the world or their community. Share what qualities make their actions significant and how those attributes can inspire personal paths to impact (1-2 minutes each).

Vision Board Snippets:

Provide magazines, scissors, glue, and paper. Have each participant create a small 'snippet' of a vision board that represents what significance looks like to them. Share and discuss the collages, exploring the various interpretations and visions of significance.

Impactful Moments Reflection:

Hand out index cards and ask each person to write down a moment in their life when they felt genuinely significant or realized the importance of their actions. Share these anonymously by mixing them up and reading them aloud. Reflect on the common themes and the diverse ways significance is experienced.

Unique Contributions Circle:

Go around the group and have each person share one unique skill or quality they possess and how they believe it can significantly impact their orbit of influence or the world. This activity helps highlight the diverse ways significance can be achieved.

GO DEEPER

Key Text: Ephesians 2:10 (NASB)

A. The Old Testament narrative is loaded with dynamic relationships. Identify two individuals whose lives (other than those discussed in this chapter) were dramatically affected by the power of words.

____

____

B. Recall incidents when words dramatically impacted your action or reaction.

____

____

____

If it was a negative experience, have you processed it healthily? If not, what steps should you take next?

____

____

If it was a positive experience, how have you paid it forward?

____

Our Capacity for Significance

Illustration to Ponder:

African wild dogs live and hunt in packs. They have a unique approach to ensuring that every pack member gets a share of the food, from the youngest pup to the oldest member. After a successful hunt, instead of gorging on their kill immediately, they will return to their den to regurgitate food for those left behind—the young, the old, or the sick.

This practice isn't limited to parents feeding their offspring, as is common in many animal species. Even non-parent adults will regurgitate food for pups that aren't their own. Their feeding strategy ensures that even those who didn't partake in the hunt directly, or those who might be too old or weak to fend for themselves, are cared for.

It's a remarkable display of social cohesion and generosity, ensuring the survival and well-being of the entire pack rather than just the fittest.

A Practical Action:

Identify two individuals within your orbit who can benefit from encouraging affirming words. Ask the Holy Spirit to show you what and when to speak into their lives.

Additional Observations:

____

____

Chapter 8
Tithing: A Gateway to Generous Living

Through the art of giving, we discover the virtuosity of living.

Because I am the Eternal One, I never change; as a result, you children of Jacob have not been destroyed though your blessing may have been delayed. From the days when your ancestors served Me, you have turned from and ignored My statutes. Return to Me and I, the Eternal, Commander of heavenly armies, will return to you. But you shameless people ask, "How will we return? Will someone steal from God?" Yet you are always stealing from Me! But you self-centered people still ask, "How have we stolen from You?" In the tithes and the offerings you have not given Me as the law requires! You are cursed with a curse, for as an entire nation you are stealing from Me. To rectify this situation, you must bring the entire tithe into the storage house in the temple so that there may be food for Me and for the Levites in My house. Feel free to test Me now in this. See whether or not I, the Eternal, Commander of heavenly armies, will open the windows of heaven to you and pour a blessing down upon you until all needs are satisfied. I will rebuke the swarm of locusts devouring your crops, and the devourer will not cause the produce you have grown in the earth to decay or the vines in the field to drop their grapes (Malachi 3:6–11 VOICE).

ICEBREAKERS

"The First Time I Tithed" Stories:

Invite members to share their first experience with tithing—what motivated them, how they felt, and what they learned. This personal sharing can illustrate the journey of faith and obedience in tithing.

Biblical Treasure Hunt:

Assign small groups to find and discuss scriptures related to tithing and generosity (e.g., Malachi 3:10, 2 Corinthians 9:6-7). This encourages engagement with the biblical basis for tithing and its role in fostering generosity.

Generosity Goals Brainstorm:

Have participants brainstorm and share one personal goal related to tithing or generosity for the upcoming month. This exercise encourages the practical application of the study's themes and mutual encouragement.

Impact Visualization:

Ask group members to visualize and describe the impact they believe their tithing can have on their church and community. Sharing these visualizations can help connect the act of tithing with its broader purpose and potential for blessing.

GO DEEPER

Key Text: Malachi 3:6–11 (The Voice)

A. Malachi challenges the people by saying they are robbing God. How do you view tithing and giving offerings in your life? As an obligation, an act of worship, or something else?

____

____

B. God challenged the people to test Him by bringing the full tithe into the storehouse. How do you feel about "testing" God in this manner?

____

____

C. Do you believe that everything you possess ultimately belongs to God? How does this belief shape your attitude toward giving?

____

____

Illustration to Ponder:

The harvester ant species are known for their diligent foraging and food storage behaviors. When they discover a food source, they don't consume it all at once. They carry a significant portion back to their nest. This food is stored in granaries, ensuring the colony sustains when food is scarce, like during the rainy season or when conditions aren't optimal for foraging. In a way, these ants *tithe* by not consuming all they find immediately. They set aside a portion for the future, ensuring the survival and well-being of the entire colony.

In a tithing context, the ants' behavior can illustrate the principle of not consuming everything we have now but setting a portion aside for the communal or greater good, ensuring that needs are met in the future or in times of scarcity.

Practical Actions:

1. Examine your current financial expenditures. If you don't have a budget, now might be a good time to create one. Understand where your money is going and how it is being used.

2. Aim to reach the 10% tithe and beyond. Consider increasing your giving incrementally. For instance, aim to increase your charitable giving by 2% in the next year and gradually increase as you become more comfortable trusting God's provision.

Additional Observations:

____

____

____

____

Chapter 9
Cultivating Authentic Relationships

Generosity generates passion in relationships.

Whoever brings blessing will be enriched and one who waters will himself be watered (Proverbs 11:25 ESV).

ICEBREAKERS

The "One Thing" Share:

Ask each group member to share one thing most people don't know about them. This can reveal unique aspects of each person's life, leading to deeper connections and breaking down barriers to authentic relationships.

Common Ground Search:

Divide the group into smaller teams and give them a few minutes to find three to five things they all have in common (beyond surface-level similarities, like being human or living in the same city). This will promote unity and show how even diverse groups have shared experiences or feelings.

Emotion Charades:

Write down various emotions on paper and have participants draw and act them out without speaking. Others guess the emotion. This light-hearted game can open discussions about expressing and identifying feelings, a key component of authentic relationships.

Trust Circles:

In a safe space, have one person stand in the center of a small circle formed by their peers. The peers gently support the person as they lean back, trusting the group to keep them upright. Rotate so each person has a turn. Debrief about the experience of trust and vulnerability in relationships.

Appreciation Round:

Each person shares an appreciation or compliment about the person to their right, focusing on character qualities rather than physical attributes. This exercise builds positive feelings and helps people see the good in each other, fostering a supportive environment for authentic relationships.

GO DEEPER

Key Text: Proverbs 11:25 (ESV)

A. Solomon said, "Whoever brings blessing will be enriched, and one who waters will himself be watered (Proverbs 11:25 ESV). Explore what it means to "bring blessing" and "water" others. Discuss examples of generosity in everyday life—helping others, sharing resources, offering emotional support, etc.

B. Delve into being "enriched" and "watered" ourselves. Discuss how this enrichment is not always material but can be emotional, spiritual, or relational. Look at biblical characters who were blessed because of their generosity, such as the story of the Widow's Offering (Mark 12:41–44). Share an experience where acts of generosity led to unexpected blessings or growth.

____

____

Illustration to Ponder:

Cuckoo birds do not build their own nests. Instead, the female cuckoo lays her eggs in the nests of other bird species, a behavior known as brood parasitism. She is very sneaky about this and waits until the host bird is away from the nest to lay her egg among the host's eggs quickly.

The cuckoo egg is often disguised to resemble the host's eggs to reduce the chances of the host bird noticing the intruder. When the cuckoo chick hatches, it instinctively pushes the other eggs or young birds out of the nest. This ruthless strategy ensures that the cuckoo chick receives all the food and care from the unsuspecting foster parents.

The host birds tirelessly feed and care for the cuckoo chick, often at the expense of their offspring. In some cases, the cuckoo chick grows much larger than its adoptive parents, yet the host birds continue to feed and nurture it, oblivious that it's not their own.

This behavior of the cuckoo bird can be seen as selfish because it benefits at the expense of the host birds. The cuckoo ensures its offspring's survival and success while jeopardizing the host birds' reproductive success. The cuckoo's brood parasitism strategy is a fascinating example of how selfish behavior can be a successful survival tactic in the natural world.

A Practical Action

Brainstorm ways to collectively participate in generosity, creating a ripple effect of blessing in your community.

Additional Observations:

____

____

____

____

Chapter 10
Holy Actions

Holy actions are redemptive deeds proclaiming the present nature of God's Kingdom.

We know love by this, that He laid down His life for us; and we ought to lay down our lives for the brothers and sisters. But whoever has worldly goods and sees his brother or sister in need, and closes his heart against him, how does the love of God remain in him? Little children, let's not love with word or with tongue, but in deed and truth (1 John 3:16–18 NASB).

ICEBREAKERS

"Act It Out" Scenario Challenge:

Create scenarios requiring moral or ethical decisions (e.g., finding a wallet or witnessing bullying). In small groups, participants demonstrate holy actions by acting out how they would respond in each scenario. After each skit, discuss alternative actions and their potential impacts.

Holy Actions Bingo:

Prepare bingo cards with different holy actions listed in each square (e.g., volunteering, praying for someone, offering forgiveness). Participants mark off actions they've done recently. The first to get a line shares one of their experiences. This game highlights the variety of ways one can live out their faith.

The Saints Among Us:

Ask each person to think of someone they know (or know of) who exemplifies living a life of holy actions and briefly describe why. This can include people from the Bible, saints, or individuals from their own lives. Discuss what qualities make their actions holy and how they can inspire our own actions.

Commitment Cards:

Provide each participant with a small card. Ask them to prayerfully consider one holy action they feel called to commit to in the coming week (e.g., an act of service, a step towards reconciliation, etc.). Participants can share their commitment with the group or keep it private. Revisit these commitments in a future meeting to share experiences and reflections.

GO DEEPER

Key Text: 1 John 3:16–18 (NASB)

A. Ecclesiastes 2:26, *God gives wisdom, knowledge, and joy to those who please him* (NLT). Hebrews 13:16 teaches us not to neglect, to do good, and to share what we have with others. Such sacrifices are pleasing to God. Identify at least two more scriptures that speak to this matter.

____

____

B. The Bible teaches that when we trust the Lord, Joy flows into our lives. Psalm 40:4, "Oh, the joys of those who trust the Lord" (NLT). This Psalm is just one scripture among many that teaches this profound truth. God, who is more powerful than we can comprehend, has promised *joy* will be a by-product of *trust*. How does this promise relate to the core theme discussed throughout this chapter?

____

____

C. Being anxious about *lack* in life indicates our relationship with God may be lacking, that our trust is linked to something or someone else. This is observable in the life of Lot (Genesis 13). Abraham and his nephew, Lot, had built significant enterprises by working side by side for decades. At a certain point, their family cooperative had reached its limits. The land where their cattle grazed could not support both their herds. Tensions increased among their herdsmen. They needed more space.

Nothing is evil about that situation, but while attempting to resolve their impasse, a nasty *agent* reared its head—greed. Lot demanded what appeared to be the best grazing area. "Lot looked about him and saw that the plain of the Jordan was well watered everywhere like the garden of the Lord ... So, Lot chose all the plain of the Jordan." Abraham allowed Lot to choose his preferred grazing territory. Abraham was not anxious regarding Lot's decision. He knew he could completely trust God whether God allowed his herds to thrive or diminish. What were the outcomes of their choices?

____

____

____

Illustration to Ponder:

Conservationist Lawrence Anthony developed a reputation as "the elephant whisperer." He could calm down African elephants. He worked in the Thula Thula Reserve, where he spent his time trying to soothe elephants that were unhappy about having been relocated there. The elephants wanted to leave, but he kept them in place, knowing they would be killed if they left the protected area. Years later, Anthony died of a heart attack. When it happened, he had not been in the reserve or seen the elephants for one and a half years. The elephants, sensing that Anthony had passed, left the reserve and traveled for 12 hours to his home to pay their respects. Just as an elephant will mourn the death of its own species, they came out for Anthony. Two entire herds of elephants came in a procession to his home. This massive group of gigantic elephants waited on Anthony's property for two days to mourn his death before they headed back home.

A Practical Action

Ask the Holy Spirit to reveal further where you need to develop your generosity. Maybe you need to be more intentional in expressing thankfulness. Perhaps you should practice being merciful to someone you have been reluctant to extend mercy to. Listen for the Holy Spirit's prompting to loosen your grip on your resources. Document the journey. In the future, you will be glad to reflect on how God led you to be generous.

Additional Observations:

____

____

____

Facilitator's Guide: Sample Answers Key

The responses below offer examples of potential answers to the discussion questions presented throughout the book. These are meant to serve as a helpful reference, especially for busy facilitators who may need quick access to insights or talking points. It's important to note that these are not exhaustive; participants may bring many other valid interpretations and ideas to the discussion. Facilitators are encouraged to explore and acknowledge diverse perspectives, using these examples as a starting point to inspire deeper conversation and engagement.

Chapter 1- Fearful to Fearless

Question A.

Colossians 3:1-17 outlines specific steps believers should follow to align with their new nature in Christ. These steps emphasize the transformation of one's mind, heart, and behavior to reflect the character of Christ.

1. Seek Things Above (Colossians 3:1-2)

- Focus your heart and mind on eternal, heavenly matters, not earthly or temporary concerns. This means living with a Christ-centered perspective, prioritizing spiritual values and eternal truths rather than the fleeting desires of the world.

2. Recognize Your New Identity in Christ (Colossians 3:3-4)

- Understand that your life is now fully identified with Christ. This means that the old self, with its sinful tendencies, has "died," and your new life is united with Christ. Living authentically starts with embracing this new identity and recognizing that our ultimate hope is in the future glory with Christ.

3. Put to Death Earthly Desires (Colossians 3:5-9)

- Actively eliminate sinful behaviors and desires that belong to your old life. This includes internal sins (e.g., lust, greed, anger) and external actions (e.g., slander, lying). Living authentically requires rejecting behaviors that are inconsistent with your identity in Christ.

4. Put on the New Self (Colossians 3:10-11)

- Embrace the process of renewal in Christ. The new self is continually being transformed to reflect God's image. This renewal is rooted in knowledge of God and transcends earthly divisions and identities. Living authentically involves allowing God to renew and reshape your character.

5. Clothe Yourself with Christlike Virtues (Colossians 3:12-14)

- Intentionally develop and practice virtues that reflect Christ's character, such as compassion, kindness, humility, patience, and forgiveness. Love is the crowning virtue that holds everything together. Living authentically means treating others with the grace and love that Christ has shown you.

6. Let Christ's Peace Rule in Your Heart (Colossians 3:15)

- Allow Christ's peace to govern your heart and relationships. This peace leads to unity within the body of Christ and promotes gratitude. Living authentically fosters peace within yourself and others, rejecting conflict and division.

7. Let the Word of Christ Dwell Richly in You (Colossians 3:16)

- Immerse yourself in Christ's teachings, allowing His Word to guide your life. This includes studying Scripture, worshipping, and encouraging one another with spiritual wisdom. Living authentically means being rooted in the truth of God's Word and allowing it to shape your actions and attitudes.

8. Do Everything in the Name of Christ (Colossians 3:17)

- Ensure that every aspect of your life—words and actions—reflects Christ. This means living in a way that honors Jesus in every situation. Living authentically means understanding that your life is a testimony of Christ to others.

Question B.

Two similar examples in the Bible where individuals relinquish something vital and, in return, discover more outstanding provision or life are:

1. The Boy with Five Loaves and Two Fish (John 6:1-14)

- In the story of the feeding of the 5,000, a boy offers his small lunch—just five loaves of bread and two fish—when Jesus asks if anyone has food to share. Though the boy's offering seems insignificant, it is all he has. Jesus takes the small offering, blesses it, and miraculously multiplies it to feed thousands. The boy's willingness to give up his food leads to a miraculous provision that meets the crowd's needs and results in an abundance of leftovers. This teaches that when we give what little we have to God, He can multiply it beyond our expectations.

2. The Offering of the Poor Widow (Mark 12:41-44)

- In this story, Jesus observes people giving offerings at the temple, and He notices a poor widow who puts in two small coins—everything she has. Though her contribution is monetarily insignificant compared to others, Jesus commends her as giving more than everyone else because she gave all she had. Her sacrificial giving becomes a model of true generosity and faith. The widow's relinquishment of all her financial resources highlights the biblical principle that God values the heart behind the gift more than the amount given. This story reflects a trust in God's provision, even when all material means are given up.

Both examples, like the widow in 1 Kings 17, demonstrate that surrendering what little we have in faith can lead to God's abundant provision and renewed joy.

Chapter 2 - Scrap Your Plans: God Has Bigger Ones

Question A.

Two more examples of similar teachings.

- Matthew 6:1-4: Jesus teaches that giving to the needy should be done without seeking public recognition. This self-abandonment in giving ensures that the reward comes from God, not from human praise, mirroring the selfless nature of Christ's service.

- Philippians 2:3-8: Paul encourages believers to have the same mindset as Christ, who humbled Himself by becoming obedient to death, even death on a cross. This passage teaches self-abandonment through humility, considering others more significant than oneself, and living a life that seeks to serve God's purposes rather than personal gain.

Question B

- King David: David exemplified a life lived for the glory of God, as seen in his passion for worship, his desire to build a temple for the Lord (2 Samuel 7), and his heartfelt prayers in the Psalms (Psalm 27:4, Psalm 63:1-5). Even when he sinned, his repentance showed his deep desire to restore his relationship with God and continue glorifying Him.

- The Apostle Paul: Paul's entire life after his conversion was dedicated to glorifying God through preaching the gospel and building up the early church (Philippians 1:21). Despite enduring tremendous suffering and persecution (2 Corinthians 11:24-28), he found joy in serving Christ and saw his life as a sacrifice for the advancement of God's kingdom, showing that his chief aim was to glorify God and enjoy His presence.

Chapter 3 - Uncomfortably Obedient

Question A.

- Illustrated Answer: Trusting God rather than relying on my understanding has taught me to be patient when I don't see an immediate solution. For example, when I faced uncertainty about a job change, I prayed and sought God's guidance instead of making a quick decision based on salary and location. This led to a workplace where I could be a witness to others.

Question B.

- Illustrated Answer: I felt God asking me to reach out to a neighbor I barely knew, someone who had recently lost their spouse. It was a little uncomfortable at first, but I sensed that God wanted me to offer comfort and support during their grieving process.

- Illustrated Answer: I sensed God prompting me to give more consistently to my church, even when finances were tight. It wasn't easy, but I felt an inner conviction to trust God with my resources, believing He would provide for my needs.

Chapter 4 - The Storm Which Released A Blessing

Question A.

- Matthew 6:33: This teaching emphasizes that when we prioritize God's Word and kingdom, trusting Him even during times of need, God will provide abundantly for our physical and spiritual needs, much like the concept of a hundredfold return.

- Luke 6:38: Jesus taught that when we give generously, whether mercy, forgiveness, or material resources, God will ensure that we receive in abundance, reflecting the principle of yielding a great return through faith.

Question B.

- Romans 10:17: This verse teaches that immersing ourselves in the Word of God is a crucial method for growing our faith. We build a deeper trust in His character, even in difficult seasons, by continually listening to and meditating on God's promises.

- James 1:2-4: James teaches that enduring trials and embracing them as opportunities for growth helps to strengthen our faith. By persevering through challenges, our trust in God becomes more resilient, even when resources are scarce.

Chapter 5 - Generosity: A Mode of Spiritual Warfare

Question A.

- The struggle between the flesh and the Spirit can be seen when believers face opportunities to give generously. The flesh might prompt thoughts like, "I need to hold onto my resources for myself," or "What if I don't have enough later?" This mindset resists giving freely, driven by fear and self-preservation. However, the Spirit encourages believers to trust in God's provision and to give freely, recognizing that true generosity reflects God's heart and blesses others. This internal conflict requires believers to consciously follow the Spirit's lead, even when it goes against their natural inclinations.

- This conflict is also evident when it comes to forgiving others. The flesh might insist on holding grudges, nurturing bitterness, and seeking revenge, while the Spirit prompts believers to extend grace and forgive as they have been forgiven in Christ. In this case, Generous living means letting go of offenses and seeking reconciliation, which can be a struggle because it requires surrendering personal pride and allowing the Spirit's power to soften one's heart.

Question B.

- Romans 8:5- 6: This passage teaches that the key to overcoming the struggle between the flesh and the Spirit is to focus on the things of the Spirit consciously. We empower the Spirit's influence by filling our thoughts with God's Word, prayer, and spiritual truths, leading to a life marked by peace and spiritual vitality.

- Ephesians 5:18: This verse encourages believers to be continuously filled with the Holy Spirit, allowing His presence to guide their thoughts, words, and actions. Being filled with the Spirit involves a daily surrender to God's will, asking Him to empower us for godly living, and seeking His direction in all aspects of life, including the choice to live generously and in alignment with God's character.

Chapter 6 - The Fruit of Generosity

Question A.

1. Ruth and Boaz (Ruth 2-4)

- Ruth, a Moabite woman, left her homeland to care for her mother-in-law, Naomi, after the death of her husband. She demonstrated loyalty and self-sacrifice by staying with Naomi and working hard to provide for them. Ruth began gleaning in the fields of Boaz, a wealthy landowner who, seeing her hard work and kindness, showed her favor. He allowed her to glean more than usual, offering her protection and special treatment. Later, Boaz married Ruth, redeeming her family line, and Ruth became the great-grandmother of King David.

2. The Generosity of the Macedonian Churches (2 Corinthians 8:1-5)

- In the New Testament, Paul highlights the churches in Macedonia (Philippi, Thessalonica, Berea) as examples of incredible generosity. Even though they were in extreme poverty and suffering, they gave generously and willingly to help the believers in Jerusalem who were facing hardship. Their generosity was not based on abundance but on their deep faith and love for fellow believers.

Question B.

1. The Practice of Sitting Shiva (Judaism)

- In Jewish culture, when a person dies, the family observes a seven-day mourning period called Shiva. During this time, mourners sit at home, and friends and community members visit them. The emphasis is often on silent presence, offering support without speaking unless the mourner wishes to talk. This tradition is similar to Job's friends sitting in silence for seven days, as it demonstrates the importance of being present without needing explanations or solutions.

2. Quiet Sitting with the Bereaved (Various African Cultures)

- In many African cultures, when a family is grieving, the community gathers to sit with them silently. This practice, sometimes called "keeping vigil," involves quietly sitting with the family, often through the night. The emphasis is not on talking but on offering physical presence and solidarity. This tradition aligns with the idea of being there without needing to fill the silence, much like Job's friends who sat with him during his suffering.

Chapter 7 - Our Capacity for Significance

Question A.

1. Joshua and Moses (Deuteronomy 31:7-8)

Before his death, Moses spoke powerful words of affirmation and encouragement to Joshua as he prepared to lead the Israelites into the Promised Land. Moses, the great leader of Israel, passed on the mantle of leadership with words that empowered Joshua to rise to the challenge.

"Be strong and courageous, for you shall go with this people into the land that the LORD has sworn to their fathers to give them, and you shall put them in possession of it. It is the LORD who goes before you.

He will be with you; he will not leave you or forsake you. Do not fear or be dismayed." (Deuteronomy 31:7-8, ESV).

These words gave Joshua confidence, strength, and courage to take on the immense responsibility of leading the Israelites. Moses affirmed Joshua's ability and assured him of God's continued presence, which was vital as Joshua faced battles and challenges ahead. This encouragement helped Joshua excel in his leadership role, leading the people into their inheritance.

2. Barak and Deborah (Judges 4:6-7, 14)

When Israel was oppressed by King Jabin and his army commander Sisera, the prophetess Deborah called upon Barak to lead Israel into battle. Barak was hesitant and lacked confidence in going to battle alone, but Deborah's words of affirmation and encouragement empowered him to rise to the challenge.

"Has not the LORD, the God of Israel, commanded you, 'Go, gather your men at Mount Tabor, taking 10,000 from the people of Naphtali and the people of Zebulun. And I will draw out Sisera, the general of Jabin's army, to meet you by the river Kishon with his chariots and his troops, and I will give him into your hand'?" (Judges 4:6-7, ESV) Then Deborah said to Barak, "Up! For this is the day the LORD has given Sisera into your hand. Does not the LORD go out before you?"
(Judges 4:14, ESV)

Despite his initial hesitation, Barak was emboldened by Deborah's words. Her affirmation that God had already given the victory to Barak and her reminder that the Lord was going before him gave Barak the courage to lead the Israelites into battle. Encouraged by her prophetic leadership, Barak excelled in his military role, leading Israel to a decisive victory over Sisera's army.

Chapter 8 - Tithing: A Gateway to Generous Living

(Questions are Personal Reflections)

Chapter 9 - Cultivating Authentic Relationships

(Questions are Personal Reflections)

Chapter 10 - Holy Actions

Question A.

1. Micah 6:8 (ESV)

"He has told you, O man, what is good; and what does the LORD require of you but to do justice, and to love kindness, and to walk humbly with your God?"

This verse teaches that pleasing God involves justice, kindness, and humility. These actions reflect a heart that seeks to align with God's will and are seen as sacrifices that please Him.

2. Colossians 3:23-24 (ESV)

"Whatever you do, work heartily, as for the Lord and not for men, knowing that from the Lord you will receive the inheritance as your reward. You are serving the Lord Christ."

These verses remind believers that whatever they do with sincerity and excellence for the Lord pleases Him. They highlight that our work and service to others, when done as unto God, bring Him pleasure and result in His reward.

Question B

Trust and Joy as Motivation for Holy Actions

- Trusting God does more than produce joy—it also motivates us to continue living holy lives. The joy from trusting God becomes a source of strength, propelling us to keep engaging in holy actions, even when the road is tough. As Nehemiah 8:10 reminds us, "The joy of the Lord is your strength." When we experience joy through trust, it strengthens our resolve to keep acting in ways that honor God.

Question C

Lot's Choice and Its Consequences:

- When given the option to choose, Lot focused on what appeared to be the best and most fertile land for his herds, choosing the plain of the Jordan near Sodom and Gomorrah, a place later described as wicked (Genesis 13:10-13). His choice was motivated by greed and anxiety about securing the best resources for himself, prioritizing material gain over spiritual well-being.

- Lot's decision led him into a progressively deteriorating situation. Though the land was initially prosperous, he became trapped by Sodom's wickedness. Eventually, Lot lost nearly everything when God destroyed Sodom and Gomorrah (Genesis 19). His greed led him to live in a corrupt environment, and although he was rescued by divine intervention, his legacy was marked by loss and hardship.

Abraham's Trust and Its Outcomes

- Unlike Lot, Abraham showed no anxiety over the outcome of the land dispute. He trusted that God would provide for him regardless of the land he ended up with. Rather than demand better land, he gave Lot the first choice, showing his confidence in God's sovereignty and provision.

- God rewarded Abraham's faith and trust. After Lot left, God promised Abraham all the land in every direction, declaring that it would belong to his descendants forever (Genesis 13:14-17). Abraham's legacy was one of blessing and expansion, as God's covenant with him grew and his faithfulness resulted in immense spiritual and material blessing for future generations.